SARAH BROOM lives in Auckland with her husband and three children. She returned to New Zealand in 2000 after spending seven years in the UK, studying and working in Leeds and Oxford. She has previously published a critical work, *Contemporary British and Irish Poetry: An Introduction* (Palgrave Macmillan, 2006).

NEW ZEALAND WRITING FROM CARCANET PRESS

Peter Bland
Selected Poems

Allen Curnow
Early Days Yet: New and Collected Poems
The Bells of St Babel's

Gerrie Fellows
Window for a Small Blue Child

John Gallas
The Book with Twelve Tales
Flying Carpets over Filbert Street
Grrrrr
Practical Anarchy
Star City
The Song Atlas (as editor)

Bill Manhire
Collected Poems
Lifted
South Pacific
Zoetropes: Poems 1972-82

John Needham
Departure Lounge

Gregory O'Brien
Days Beside Water
News of the Swimmer Reaches Shore

C.K. Stead
Collected Poems 1951-2006

Twenty Contemporary New Zealand Poets
Edited with an introduction by Andrew Johnston and Robyn Marsack

Tigers at Awhitu

SARAH BROOM

OxfordPoets
CARCANET

for Hilkja

Acknowledgements are due to the editors of the following journals, in which
some of these poems previously appeared: *Acumen, Bravado, brief, JAAM, Landfall,
Metre, Orbis, Oxford Poetry, Poetry New Zealand, Spin* and *Takahe*. 'The First Gesture'
was first published in the anthology *Swings and Roundabouts: Poems on Parenting*,
edited by Emma Neale. 'The Third Daughter' was first published in the 2007
New Zealand Poetry Society competition anthology.

First published in Great Britain in 2010 by
Carcanet Press Limited
Alliance House
Cross Street
Manchester M2 7AQ

First published in New Zealand in 2010 by Auckland University Press, University of
Auckland, Private Bag 92019, Auckland 1142, New Zealand

A CIP catalogue record for this book is available from the British Library
ISBN 978 1 903039 991

The publisher acknowledges financial assistance from Arts Council England

Printed and bound in England by SRP Ltd, Exeter

Contents

Snow

It was as the snow started falling again
that she blurted it out, so they were all
just standing there gazing up, knee-deep
in snow, the little one thigh-deep,
when they heard it, the news that slipped
out like a necklace from a sleeve,
not meant for the kids, not meant for here,
for the snowwoman with her pink hat
and old carrot nose, for the creaking
pines, the cracked plastic sled, the neat
rabbit tracks that shied all over the white
field. So they stood there, the little one
lost in any case in this too white world,
his too cold hands stiff in his wet wool
gloves, his feet stuck somewhere
miles down below. And once it was out
she wished she could call it back in,
like a dog you could whistle to,
but it wouldn't, you couldn't,
so they stood there in the snow,
and the big one asked, of course,
'what's that?' and his dad just looked
straight back at her, his clove-brown eyes
soft with fear, the hound's sour breath
hot on the nape of his neck.

The Butterfly House

His eyelids are itchy red.
Under each eye,
a sealed pool of grey.

In the butterfly house
his skin moistens and his breathing
starts to ease. We stay for hours
as he tiptoes in the muggy air,
peering under giant leaves
to seek out blue morphos, tailed jays,
flambeaus, lacewings, the soulful
mimic eyes of the owl butterfly.

But it is the resting atlas moth
that draws him, with its mapped,
furry wings, each tip the perfectly
painted head of a snake. Surrounded
by a glut of nectar, it cannot drink.
Without a proboscis, it lives
on its stores, then dies.

It worries him.
He knows too much
about short lives, appetite,
about time that wears
as ragged as storm-blown wings.

Boy

when I was growing up I saw
my life sprawled out in front of me
like a universe of stars, deeper
and further than I could imagine

when he looks ahead
he sees a cave, black as space

glow-worms look just like stars
but he knows they lie

he walks forward
with his hands stretched out
feeling for the end

Under the Hospital

The car motor gurgles and clicks like a nervous stomach.
Voices balloon for a few seconds in a stairwell, then a door clangs.
The air smells metallic. Neon lights hang from chains.
A fly rattles along the windscreen, and the lift whines.

I listen hard for the sound of the drip being hauled closer
to her bed, for the sound, many floors up, of the nurse's
vacant step as she changes the sheets, of the meal trolley
as it hums the packaged meals round sharp corners.

A neon light goes out. A car spins in and tyres squeak
as it angles into a park. Outside there is a granite sky
and birds are singing through the rush-hour traffic.
I can feel the impossible weight of the hospital
pressing down on the concrete ceiling: the beds,
the oxygen machines, the laundry bags, bins
for this and that, the coffee shop with its subdued muffins,
the fuzzy, dogged chairs, the mute plastic toys.

I listen harder, for the bump of her foot as it knocks
the end of the bed, for the flush of the toilet in the room
next door, for the wince in her breath as she tries to turn,
for the hiss of fear in the recirculating air.

Spring

For a while it hurt, how every year
the spring galloped in. Orange flowers crowded
my study window, the scent forced its way in
through the cracks. In a matter of days
a twitch of green became a riot of leaves.
The banal, insulting ease of it.

Meanwhile, degeneration.
I could not find the spring inside me
any more. My body was faulting all over
like a badly wired circuit. I looked
at the children with their apple tree eyes,
their honeysuckle skin, their sappy,
yawning mouths, and I hated them.

But eventually I gave up on it,
kicked it away, my body, the wreck,
the fantasy. And then it started.
Daffodils sprouting between my toes.
Fantails nesting in my beard. Blossom
in my navel, daisies in my groin.
Baby rabbits sleeping in my dressing gown
pockets. And the smells on the breeze
that wafted around my head! I let it be.
Usually people go out with the winter,
but I had a feeling that spring
would take care of me.

North

i

The ground will not let us in. The sky
has shut us out. And so we step
in and out of sleep between ground
and sky, walking into the shapeless north.
The ruts of other carts are frozen hard.
The road is lumpy with dropped hats,
dolls, worn-out shoes, the things that
got too much or were no use.
We think all the time of the boat.
We do not think about what lies behind.
When it snows we think that snow
at sea level is very rare. When a pine
crashes down in our path and we struggle
to haul our cart over it we think of the wood
that's used for shipbuilding, the clatter
of boots on the timber deck, the honey
varnish of the curved interior walls.
When we lie down to sleep at night,
tenting ourselves against the indifference
of the stars, we think of the slow swell
of the sea, of being rocked to sleep
and forgetfulness in the warm belly
of the ship that waits in the north.

ii

The forested, snow-dusted hills
are as grey as a stubbly chin.
A hawk turns in the white sky, and we lie
like carrion, a rough scrawl of limbs on the road.

Everest

the frozen man
sits in the ice cave
hunched
like a beggar
by the side of the road

the frozen man
sees the headlamps
coming
disco lights
spinning

the frozen man
throws himself at the voices
hurls himself down the mountain

the frozen man
is in a very small place
in the middle of his head
that is still warm

he is six
and he is in his brother's bed
arguing about what they will make
for their mother's birthday
it is belly dark under the blanket
and his brother's toenails are sharp

the frozen man
tries to reach out to his warm brother
but his limbs are as heavy
as the old oak bedposts

it is dawn now on the mountain
the blunt sun slumps low in the sky
the rocks resume their vigil
and a cracked wind blows

Delta

she sits and swings her legs
looks down at the mud
up at the moon
waiting for the late boat
that will bring him home

the flood tide will come
when the moon is full

plump, brown and insatiable,
the river has gathered water
from the unleashed glaciers,
the intemperate sky

a dip of her finger in the bucket
the groundwater is saltier every day

the river probes and sucks
at the edges of the char
mangroves clutch and claw
in the silt

boats come and go as darkness
slouches down to the water

a few more days till
the moon is full

somewhere deep in the Sundarbans
waking up to the yellow-eyed night
sniffing the briny air
the tigers are thirsty

The Third Daughter

from outside, the slow voices of men
draped in afternoon shadow

through the mud wall
the whispering of women

dried ginger hot under the tongue
the rattle of rice
at the bottom of the bucket

sleep crawls around me
and over me but I am afraid
and nudge it off

moulded to my body she drowses,
her breath on my throat
as slight as swaying grass

my hunger is sharp but food is scarce
and the women are pressing their point

have they gathered the oleander?

*

the dry lick of warm skin
the emptiness of air
soft hands and hard hands
the stumbling up and down of talk
that voice

*

my body aches to her

but there is a strangeness about newborns,
a distance which can be groomed away
bit by bit, or grasped and held
to bear the unbearable

when they come in
their faces are sewn up tight
and as they start to talk I can only stare
at the papery nails on her curled
fingers, the red-veined shells
of her closed, unbidden eyes

*

I am a land picked over and over by birds

now everything is dust

Leviticus

you must keep the Israelites

The pigeons were loud on the rooftops,
it was hot, and there was trouble on the streets.
At night I slept holding her tight in my arms.
In the daytime we dozed, the two of us,
in the courtyard under the pomegranate tree.

separate from things that make them unclean

For the first fourteen days,
and then thirty-three days after that,
I was happy not to go to the temple,
I didn't want to go anywhere,
I wanted to curl up with her
in the ochre light that enveloped us
like two seeds in a sun-drunk fruit.

so they will not die

But then a sulky, muscular wind started up,
sand began to blow in the courtyard,
and the air turned grey as an old rag.
The woman next door, whose boy
had been born just after my girl,
went off to the temple to be made clean.

in their uncleanness

I looked at my body, still slack and heavy,
and at my daughter, with her thirsty soil-brown eyes.
Who was it that could not look at me
because she reminded them so much of death?

for defiling my dwelling place

When my sixty-six days were up
I took my two doves and two pigeons
to the priest, and as he killed them neatly
for the offering – one burnt offering, one sin offering –
I thought about how clean she was when she was born,
how her skin never seemed to need washing,
how her forehead smelled of life compacted, distilled,
and how strange it was that because of her
someone wanted blood.

which is among them
among them

Twins

The smell of goat meat cooking
always made him queasy. Sometimes
he woke at night with its cloying fog
in his nostrils and the soft slip
of fresh goat hide on his skin.

In dreams he saw his red-haired,
impetuous brother as he used to be
when he came back from the hunt, laughing,
exhausted, flinging an arm round his shoulder.
But in the dreams the laughs
turned to screams and hacking coughs
and Esau was sick and mad.

It worried him, the way
he'd got started, the fact that God
had stuck by the liar. But he prospered,
couldn't put a foot wrong. So when
he returned with his wives,
servants and children, he sent
herds of animals in front of him as gifts –
goats, sheep, camels, cows and donkeys –
and when that night he wrestled
with a stranger by the river
it was the matted hair of his brother
that he felt on the muscled arm
of the angel, and the stranger's skin
had the rough, sweet smell of Esau
that was all he knew of home.

Crusade

And I wondered what kind of a thing the soul was –

was it me turned inside out?

And if you took the wrecked walls, the heads on poles,
the mosaics slippery with blood, the dead horses,
the hunger, and turned it all inside out,
what would you get?

The held breath of an angel?

Or the death rattle
of a coin belt ripped
from the waist of a dying man.

All my life

So we sat, and the waves
crashed in like gifts, or insults,
and the children played,
digging trenches to defend
against the sea, and then a head
bobbed up and down
in the waves, a bit too far out,
and an arm waved, and again,
and a friend walked the beach,
waving the head in, and we sat
and said to each other
do you know that Stevie Smith
poem, not waving but drowning –
yes, and why is it still so hard to tell,
and then we stood and watched
as the inscrutable head bobbed up
and down and the arm still waved
and the children still dug, bodies
roughcast with sunscreen and sand,
and we thought about getting the
lifeguards, but surely the friend
should know, and we thought
about how there should be a sign,
you know, two punches in the air,
or something like that, yes,
then a surfer came and paddled
him in on his board, and the friend
helped him walk, and yes he was
drowning, not waving, now we know,
and isn't it hard to tell?

Monochrome

The beach is heaped and hilled with bleached branches
as if whole forests have been rolled over the ocean
and dumped. He picks his way over the clutter,
through the glare of wood and stone.
The stones are all much larger
than they should be, the beach is heavier
than any beach he has ever known.

Darkness now and they are blind clumsy creatures,
tripping over logs and falling in ditches as they stumble
over the fields towards the beach, the baby lurching on a hip.

And in the ditches the darkness is different,
thick and soft, like the spawning of blame.

At the bonfire black shapes hulk in rain jackets and the sky
spits darkly. The wind blows the taste of salt
into their mouths, and the older kids run off in the dark
until their voices fray in the wind.
The fire is fed with more pale skeletons,
whole forests burning.

Her face is pulled as tight as a snagged line. His eyes
are as cold as the juddering sea. They are sullen, mutual quarry.
There's something about a jacket, or maybe a hat,
something, again, has been left behind.

Fosterling

Floating upwards he gazes
at the quiver of blue and the crush
of white bubbles from the kids' kicking feet.
He surfaces, feels the naked slap
of air on his face, and dives again,
right down into the cushioned deep.
Turns like a seal, letting himself rise slowly,
eyes so wide open they hurt. And again. And again.

well, it brings a bit more money in, doesn't it?
he's not much trouble either, poor bugger,
dead quiet, actually

In the room with the laminated Concorde picture
he peels the wallpaper systematically,
strip by tiny strip. His pillow
feels rough as pavement on his cheek.

ah, the other kids'll be ok with him.
they do their thing at first, you know,
show him what's what,
but then they settle down

On his back he feels a hand stroking
and then the absence of the hand. He bites
down hard on the old blanket
he has carried from place to place.
Who gave it to him?
He bites till his teeth ache.

yeah, got the social worker coming round tomorrow
won't have any hassle though, cos the kid hardly talks
far as I can tell

He is underwater again, but this time
there's no need to rise for air. He sinks
and sinks. The kicking feet
are frothy seagulls in a lean blue sky.

What happens

Blackfriars Bridge to the South Bank,
metal grill pounding, the turbid Thames below

pause, dripping, in the sudden vaulting gloom
of the Turbine Hall

him, in the crush of wet coats and plates
and coffee cups

Sunday afternoon,
paint-mottled, reptilian skin
the smack and shine of paint in the air
the bashful sun brushing the floor

and then this girl

who bolts around the room
like a crazy colt, who wants a naked party
for her third birthday, who throws herself
with blue abandon into the deep end of the pool,
who is obsessed with the sea and all its creatures
gannets, dolphins, stingrays, orcas,
so far from the sea

who sleeps now
with dark hair falling over her face,
lips parted, cheeks like anemones
ears soft crumpled shells

She walks through the house

feet soft as clouds on the wooden floor
eyes licking the shadows

the kitchen has a cool obsidian gleam
and the windows are sheets of water
you could put your hand through
to feel the night

the glitter and purr
of cream on dark water
the shush and sweep
of tiny waves

she listens for the baby's breath,
the swish of a moth's wings
on a pillow

the sand is cold at night

her fingers are long and pale,
fluttering over her stomach
as she hunts for the bite

the thrash of white
in the rocking sea

Scarecrow and Crow

The small child in the big hat
stands on the prickly grass. The hot
sky sighs and lets its weight fall
on the small child in the big hat
who stands on the prickly grass.

Gaunt crows caw at his back,
the parakeets cackle and screech
and the trees gossip dryly
about the small child in the big hat
who stands on the prickly grass.

I am the maimed scarecrow,
wind-riddled, giddy with the shock
of air in straw, face flapping open,
limbs splintered and askew. It looks
as though I'll be left this way,

open to the plunging sun,
open to the ransacking wind,
left to the sidling caws of the crow
whose claws dig deep
into the shudder of my spine.

Echoes

that's where the echoes live!

the dry litter of leaves over the grating
the hot scutter and shine of gecko

O yes, it's true, the echoes live here
and everywhere

here in the cracked sun and concrete heat
but also in the steep creek
where the blind vines get you by the throat,
the rotten wood collapses in its heart as you touch,
and the mossed rocks slither under your feet

there, it's a slow clear trickle
into pools of dark water,
and if you put your face close
to the mud and mulch
you can hear
the breath of the dead

Heat

dry attic blast
of heat from the hatch
clatter and menace of rats in the night

helicopter! you shout, and we raise our eyes,
slowly, to the sun

the plums simmer endlessly on the stove,
bruising the air with sweetness

your little planes succumb to the glaze,
lose their cool
in these days of wrenched metal,
slivers of glass in the sofa

kangaroo plane! we lift our heads
to the splintered sky

on the windowsill, candles slump
in the sun, their ends
like amputated limbs

there is only room for the languid
drifting planes, the cicadas' blistered rasp
and your red plum-skinned hands

skin on skin

at night, your breath comes fast and sweet

Displacement

Like that time when my son called out to me
and my reply caught and died, gorse-choked, in my throat,
as I heard a voice, somewhere in the house,
answer in my stead. A voice like mine,
but harder, rougher, more real than me,
and I felt ghostly, supplanted, insubstantial,
and had to steady the lurch inside me
before trying out my voice and my step
like a miner standing in rubble and darkness
testing each limb and tasting the dust on his lips.

The First Gesture

The first gesture is a reaching out,
arms awkwardly extended,
flailing a little in the treacherous space
between us. His eyes invoke
the perfect arrangement of bodies,
the reciprocal movement of the pole star.
It starts as willed action – he's trying
to move to me – but in the failure of action
it slips into gesture, symbol,
which works like a miracle.

As I was trying to say it all
as the metal gate slammed shut
behind us, as the skittering parrots
tore our words to shreds
and the nor'wester blew them
back and forth between us,
gaudy scraps of cut-out people,
I thought how all our tattered talk
remembers those waving arms,
their feeble reach,
their bright and bare desire.

Red Sail

A red sail shouts out in the middle of the harbour,
a single red sail against the silver glare of sky
and water, and I point out the red sail to you – boat! –
and then turn back and catch your eye, your smile
so conspiratorial, so radiantly plump that I stay
tuned into it dangerously long, then I turn back
to the sun – shall we drive into town? – and because
you know that all questions deserve an answer,
and because you love to be part of the conversation,
you give me one of your important, definite nods,
and I laugh and drive on, and still the red sail
flares in the white, as if to say lucky, lucky
 – god, look how lucky you are.

The Island

The plump foot presses
against my rounded belly
like the mouth of tomorrow.
This is your brother, his foot
already kneading you. Notice
the insistence of his stout legs,
the way they crave something
to push against to find sleep.
Sleep that comes so slowly,
resisted to the last few seconds,
till it carries him away, eyes
rolling white, the smell
of the island of flowers,
the boat dipping in the waves,
his skin salty to taste. He wraps
a strong arm round my neck
and we gently graze the shore.

Husk

Look, Mummy, here's a picture of God!
Oh, so God looks like – a dinosaur!
Yes, but with a longer neck.

The shadow is hungry, and races
across the beach, faster
than we can move our things.

Gold hair is thickening on his legs.
In the bath alone he lengthens and lolls.

I already knowed that, I didn't need you to tell me that.

There is a steep drop below
the high tide mark. The waves
are sucked back fast like a child
being yanked back from a road.

For a while he resists the idea
that we are spinning in space.
He accepts evolution easily
with no sense of time –
of millions, of billions,
of the span of a life
like the husk of a fingernail
discarded on the ground.

The pohutukawa clings to a clump
of earth on the cliff face. Gnarled
and snaky, it grins at the sun
and plays for time.

I can't sleep tonight. I can't find out how to.

Time and space settle in slowly,
like the creeper which idles over the wall
and fingers the bedroom window.

World

it's his second day and the intercom
blares, the children dive under the desks,
it's an earthquake drill! and they all
file out on to the field to be counted
in the rain, it's just routine, it's a drill
don't you know what that means?
but his teeth begin to chatter, his face
is pale, the ground is cracking open
under his feet and he needs to go home

if you're happy and you know it
clap your hands

a black patch of sea where a boat was
and is no more, a small group of adults
huddled on rocks, staring at the patch
of sea where the boat should be, at the
black sea that swallowed the boat
and the children who couldn't get out
of the boat to swim to the black rocks
to huddle and stare at the sea till someone
comes when the black night lightens

if you're happy and you know it
clap your hands

is Rangitoto dormant or extinct? yes, it could
erupt, but it's so unlikely that we shouldn't
even think about it and yes, they do have life jackets
on planes in case they crash into the sea – it almost
never happens, but just in case. Just like the earthquake
drill – same thing, just in case. So you know what to do.

if you're happy and you know it
then your face will surely show it
if you're happy and you know it
clap your hands

Absence

The socks curl up and laugh like hyenas
on the classroom carpet. Oh he just won't go,
I can't get him to do it. Well, you can't force them,
can you? The umbrellas chatter humpily along,
and toddlers charge at puddles. Careful,
she can't go that fast! More marmite sandwiches.
Seagulls freckle the muddy field. How about a kiss?
I have to go, I have to get back for the plumbers,
they're probably waiting outside. Convoys
of sleek people-movers snuffle at the gates. Oh god,
another reliever, he's not going to like that.
The field rushes down to the water, where
thwarted boats slump in the estuary shallows.
Did she really say that? Look now,
the rain has stopped. Thin women march off
with children tightly strapped in buggies. Go on,
run now, you're going to be late! Gum trees drip
on the timid, the blithe, the fierce goodbyes.

Being

for Lynda

your skin so thin that heart and brain beat through,
soft drums undercover

sound unprocessed, uninterpreted
tiptoes in as the silken horn of the ear is finished

your tongue skitters out, samples, retreats

first light slips through the black nib of the pupil

being accretes in layers as sensations repeat,
vary, proliferate

and if, like those others, you never made it
to the big shock, the belly-flop into cold water,
the ankle-grabbing ride we call birth

what would you be?

oh, the butter on my chin, buttercup
the sheen, the shine on a lick of paint, yes luck again
the smell of rain in the air, the hair, the softest hair
the salt of tears in the crack of the lip, the hip
of the night, the nudge, the nuzzle, the nip of the light

Auction

for Alex and Jen

from the bridge you could get pulled in,
the way the stream mutters into darkness,
the trees leaning in, glossy and secretive

and do you remember?
feet sunk in mud and tangled in weed,
pushing past bushes, sneaking past curving lawns,
running hunched over through concrete pipes

slipping down with a key for the school pool,
soles fiery on hot tarmac, the clean stretch into blue

with this wide open sky
you might think it was all still here

feet marked in squares from the hard cord of the trampoline,
rose thorns stuck on noses, the maple's slow burn into red,
the squish of a foot into a rotten pear,
the private, impassable heat of your room in the afternoon sun,
the thud of balls against the garage wall,
the milky touch of the piano keys in the cool dark lounge,
the mess of bantam crap and feathers, the prickly blackcurrant bush,
the high bathroom window you dived into head first if you got locked out,
the books you had time to read over and over again,
the tomato soup, the gouged kitchen table,
the wet roses slapping the glass by the window-seat
as the rain came down and down

a bird dips its head in the fountain that was never there,
raises it sharply, and looks around

The Years

Patter and whisper
of mice on the floor.
Claw and scrape
of gorse at the door.

The bach sighs and dozes
through long, still days
till the boat arcs in
to the barnacled wharf
and it all begins again

the stealthy reek of leaked gasoline
the blundering of fish-gut hands and rock-cut feet
the rasp of the rusty slasher in the hot grass
the flap and slap of fillets on a board
the lamp's hissing lurch into night.

And now and then they leave
for the solo walk to nowhere,
around the salted rocks and back again.

The unclocked days pass slowly,
on the beach under the flared sun
or in the huddling rain, in the garrulous room
where bread swells in the stove.
The days are long and leisured
but the years, the years
pass by like the dark swoop of the stingray
as it slides under the jetty,
a fleeting shadow
in the far corner of your eye.

The Wrong Death

Hunched and jacketed, we fish
in fear of the wrong death.

Four grey shags patrol the water,
poachers, opportunists.
As we reel in, they dive.

One cod is pulled clear
with half its body in the shag's mouth,
but the bird drops off
like a dog from a torn sleeve.

We execute small deaths
with equanimity
but the shags unnerve us.
We imagine strong wings beating
against the aluminium seats,
a rusty hook in a slender throat,

a blade slitting the white sky.

Three Birds

i

The grey gull circles
in the bleached sky.
When a tune or story
splits you cleanly
like an axe to white pine,
that's when the grey gull
spirals down and you turn
your head, you turn
to see a sudden sea
behind you, vast and dark,
and the forgotten waters move
and wash over your feet
and you are unmoored,
bewildered and eased.

ii

Some people sink away into death, eyes
slow and heavy-lidded, already listening
to voices from somewhere else
like monks nodding to the clang of temple bells.
You sit in the bush before dawn,
listening to the seep of the soil, feeling
the rags of the night air on your skin.
You wait until the kokako starts to sing
in the still-dark trees, until slowly
you start to make out its ash-grey form

against the growing light. Eyes black
as the rotting leaves, and at its throat
a hurtled scrap of sky.

iii

You feel the windrush of wing and tail
as the hawk passes within a feather's breadth
of your head. In the glare you struggle
to track it as it wheels in the sun's throat
and returns to land on your shoulder,
heavy as a child, claws deep in your flesh.
There is no reason, no excuse for what has happened,
and the world stares back blankly when you hit out.
The air has been sucked out of the landscape
like water from a bathtub. The hawk
with fishhook claws tucks its head under its wing
and looks as if it might stay forever,
a welted shadow over the trench of your eyes.

Muriwai

The taut sand slips its skins
of blue and green in the half-light.

The motorbikes gouge their trails,
vicious and rhythmical,
answering the tangled surf
with a reciprocal violence,

answering the seagulls'
wheeling and circling,

spraying black sand
round each careless,
exact curve,

carving hieroglyphs
of rubber and steel,

a divulging, a matching
as they angle to the earth,

sand drifts banking on one side,
the rash sea on the other,

a measured, even space for opening up
the unmeasured, the riven, the exposed.

They take off their helmets slowly,
a startled look
in each gulled, brilliant eye.

Caving

The air is thunderous
with the earth's pent-up noise.
The water has claimed us to our waists,
we lean into and against it,
angling for a grip.

In our torchlight
the limestone walls are smooth
and carved, like sand dunes,
desert architecture,
cold to my cold touch.

When we turn off our torches,
there is only a solidarity of darkness.

This world is only ever
water, rock and black air.
It cannot accommodate us;
we cannot, will not complain
when the water deafens and knocks us.
We shut our eyes
and meet its volleyed blackness.

Words

What I meant and what she heard –
the words are like exhausted plasticine,
malleable to flickering guilts
and the punctual scares of the lucid night.
If I had changed them round,
put one in, left one out,
perhaps they would not have settled here
like moths –
the white fuzz of their cold wings
agitating the shadows.

The Cough

A streak of blood and all those scenes
from old movies wind past, you know the ones –
the destitute family struggling through the European winter,
the hacking cough, the denial, the camera zooming in
on a blood-spattered white handkerchief.

Which always means the end.
Now everything's less dramatic –
blood is just blood, and doesn't
have to mean a thing.

Still, what was it that you said?
You know you'll die like that, don't you?
And yes, it's probably true, I can see it now,
I hold it at bay all my adult life, until one year
it settles in like a cold winter, snowflakes drifting
down through all those tiny passageways,
fine as fennel or aniseed. And as the breathing
gets harder and the cough gets weaker
will I still look for meaning, pattern?
Or will I only know
the steady choking rise of the snow?

This space

We are both trapped
in this body, you and I.

There's clearly too much blood
in my veins, someone needs
to hang each limb up,
drain them out.

In the darkness
when the night kitten comes
I don't sneeze like I usually do,
she curls up between my breasts
to help me sleep. In the morning,
my skin is scaly red.

At full stretch in the water
I can't feel my body any more
and you are quiet too,
letting me pretend
I've turned into that rare
sliver of moon silk
that floats in the pool.

Once at night I thought
there was a dead rat floating
but it was just a plastic dolphin,
gaping, dark, melancholy.

When I turn on my front
and let my belly hang down
in the black water,
you give me a kick –

remember
we're in this together
don't you know

The City

At night I watch the sun set unencumbered.
It sinks into the sand like the death of the world itself.

On moonlit nights they send out cloaked messengers
from the city. They look for people like me.
They crouch down on the cold sand
and try to tempt us into argument.

The city's shadows are intricate.
Sometimes in the early morning
when they stretch out towards me
I trace them with my feet,
towers and giant round mirrors,
swooping curlicues and spikes.

Most of the time I study
the ripples in the sand,
the way the lines waver
towards each other
but never touch.
What I miss most
is the warmth
of another body.

Sometimes at dusk there are strange lights
that seep through the windows
of the stone houses and towers.
When the lights start, a swarm of small animals
flees the city, wriggling through holes
in or under the wall. A rat passed me,
heading for the open desert.

Every day a wagon heads out through the gates
into the desert with a covered load.
When it comes back it is empty.

At night I spend hours studying the stars.
I lie on my back, blanketed,
and shiver my way through the vertigo.

Once I dreamed that the city was burning
but I woke to its clotted darkness
hard at my head, pressing out the stars.

The Plain

I crawl through the long grass.
The sun is gnawing at my back.

Was that a voice?
I throw myself to the ground
and lie still, cheek to the prickly earth.

The grass is churning with insects,
and the trapped heat pulses.

My hand is slack and pink, half buried in the grass
like a sleeping animal. A spider ambles over it.

Is that the hiss of a slasher in the distance?
My chest is tight. I'm not getting much air.
I can't allow myself to cough.

I crawl forward on knees and elbows.

I think the sharp grass is talking to me,
telling me of a time when breath came easy
and cool shadows fell on the purple flowers and the dry grass
because the mountains came crouching near.

Now it is a shadowless plain
where night never falls

and everyone listens for boots in the grass.

Lie low and try to breathe.

Keep moving

I lumber over the land, knees swollen
and knotted like giant kumara roots.
Who is that child so far down below
who reaches out to me? I can barely hear
his cry, he is simply too far away. I trudge
through drying braided rivers, I step
over tussocky brown hills. What do you say,
you small people waving your hands at me
from beside the lake? You think I should stop,
you want to help, the child needs me?
Huh. No, no, the heat is its own desperate cure,
the creaking legs need to keep moving,
the dry earth knows all about me. The child?
Oh yes, I can see him still, I think he's
getting smaller – isn't that strange? Maybe
he'll disappear – meanwhile, I have my eye
on that razor pass through the mountains.
I think I may have been there before.

NO

IT'S NOT
SOMETHING WE CAN GET RID OF
TIME / GET RID OF / YOU / CAN / LIVE FOR
SOMETHING / BUT / TIME / A LOT / WE CAN / NOT
NO / YOU HAVE A LOT TO LIVE FOR / NO
IT'S NOT / TIME / TO LIVE FOR / YOU / GET RID
A LOT / IT'S NOT / BUT WE CAN GIVE YOU TIME / NOT / A LOT
TO LIVE / FOR / YOU / TO LIVE
BUT / WE CAN
NOT

BUT

Hospital Property

Because I am alone in this cold room,
because the Siemens Somatom EmotionDuo
CT scanner is about to talk to me again
and tell me, of all things, to breathe normally,
because I cannot hear right now the wind
in the pines just behind the beach, the way
it runs at night so high above your head,
because my gown says HOSPITAL PROPERTY
all over, and because someone said
BUT WE CAN GIVE YOU TIME
and someone else said WELL, YOU SEE,
IT'S NOT MY KIND OF CANCER,
and because just one fist, held close enough,
was enough to block out the light
from the giant white window where the traffic
kept travelling over and over the bridge,
and because they stuck my heart
to its lining and my lung to its lining
to stop up the gaps, and because right now
I cannot hear the wind as it probes
the gaps in the roof, rattles the corrugated
iron, and because I am about to move again,
to look at the red light circling, to be told
again to take a deep breath, again
to breathe normally, because of all this
I am not quite the same as I used to be.

No, but wait. Watch what happens now.

Ward 64

the curtain's beige and orange checks
do nothing to divide us

when her drip beeps I think it's mine

when she hears the bad news
I have to put my iPod on to keep it out

across the room he's lost his wedding ring
because he's got so thin

skinny fingers
I'd better watch out for that

there is poetry all over the walls
of oncology

and I want to get out

Three Exercises for Oncologists

1. Define false hope.

2. Explain why that hump in the centre of the bell curve makes you feel safe.

3. Design a randomised, controlled, double-blind trial to assess the efficacy of telling patients that they will die within twelve months.

What the wind does

it hunts through the forest of mangrove roots

and what else does the wind do?

it tosses flecks of foam along the sand

and what else does the wind do?

it licks my bald head with a cold tongue

and what else does the wind do?

it lunges and whines under the overturned dinghy

and what else does the wind do?

it shows me how much air is in the world

and what else does the wind do?

it ruffles the chest feathers of the strutting gull

and what else does the wind do?

it whips around my face and tells me not to die

Rain

She's been lying
on the jetty for weeks,
cheek flat on the wet
wood, mouth an inch
from a fishgut stain,
knife at her elbow.

The rain just keeps
coming down.

She's as naked
as a shucked scallop,
raw and white
on the splintered planks.

Her breath is as slight
as the sea's sway.

Up there in the bush
all the trees lean down
and inwards, longing
for the creek,
which longs
for the sea.

And the grey ocean
nuzzles the sand,
its waves as gentle
as tiny licks or kisses,
their small collapse
an everytime surrender.

Don't touch her.
Let it rain.
Let it rain.

Panther

panther water
iron black

when I turn my back
you reach for me

ah! the cold

I turn to you
I turn to you

Ectopic

What did you say your heart felt like?
O, like a fish
thrashing in a bucket.
And what shall we do with this heart,
this berserk heart?
We should watch and wait.
Should we hold her?
Yes! if we can.
Take her
in your hands
and meet
her giddy beat.

Hold it there

Why do you lie so long spread-eagled
on that red rock, cheek to its roughness?

Ah, well, you see . . .

this red rock has been blasted
by the untamed breath of the sun
licked by the rain's slow tongue
whipped by the long
tail of the wind, swallowed
by the impassive night
and then again
and again

the sun
hot breath

ahhhh

One more time now

The sweet rumble of the orthodox soul
spills over into the Melbourne street.
How could it fall right into my heart like that?

★

Look out! A bird's nest
of cranes and giggly tower blocks.

★

My soul hangs vertically in the air
like the green tea bag swaying in my mug.

★

I shut my eyes and a mass of tiny
purple flowers shower my eyelids.
So where did *they* come from, now?

★

Do me a favour, don't let me go too high.
Give me a yell every now and then
or I might just float away.

Look closely

the sand has been carved
in rivulets as fine as hairs
or capillaries or bronchioles

and as it flows the water
endlessly redraws the map,
recreates the system

fine tuning, each shift
as gentle as the brush
of your mouth on my skin

and what if the body
could be so easily moved
so tenderly readjusted

go on
move me now

A Terribly Unfair Question

and if we stood right here
while this sun, low and red,
just sank into the cradling sea,
and if we kept on standing
here, as the ragged cliffs
started to darken behind us
and the air grew rough
and unsteady with the edge
of the night, and if the earth,
instead of turning slowly
towards morning, just spun
out of orbit and went crying
into the luminous, star-stabbed
true cold of space, and if
we could still stand here
even then, with the ocean
losing its footing, the gulls
flailing and the stars
unleashed

tell me

what would you

do?

Tigers at Awhitu

i

tiger, why do you hide?

my fur is matted
and mangy, my face
is raw, there's red
under my claws

tiger, have you killed?

no, not for weeks
of stony days
and vagrant nights

tiger, why do you cry?

I cannot say

I think my heart
was left unwatched
and opened,
secretly, rashly,
like a flower in the night

sleep, tiger, sleep
sleep and let it be

tiger hearts can take a lot

of love

ii

Tigers at Awhitu? I don't think so.

Ah, but you should have seen her!

Tearing along the beach like nobody's
business, scrambling up those sand dunes,
sitting all dignified at the top staring out
over the Tasman, whiskers delicately
waving in the wind. And hurtling down,
paws wild and lost. Lying panting
at the bottom, her fur dense with sand,
eyes laughing like only a tiger's can.

Honestly, love, I saw it all myself.

iii

A throaty growl
like the first kick
of the outboard motor.

Easy, tiger.
I know you're there.

iv

There's a gouge in the dining-room table.
The sofa cushions are torn to shreds.
Tiger's on the rampage again. Fuck! Get out!

v

I hid three cubs
in a green den
and when I returned
the grass smelt only
of their terror.

vi

She bats your head between soft paws,
her tail is firmly coiled around your calf.
She's long and lazy, greedy for sun
like bread dough left out to rise. She rubs
her ear against you, slow as love.
Her whiskers tickle your chin. Come on
now, open your eyes, don't let this go.

vii

Tiger, when the world is wild
what do you do?

I pick up my tail and follow it.

I hunt the hiss at the back of the wind,
track the bird with the crooked beak, trail
the tremor that wants to crack the earth
beneath my paws. I sniff out the places
where hunger thrives and stalk the shadow
that seeks to hide my face, my yellow eyes.

And when I have found enough wildness
I lie down right inside it

and sleep.

Not yet, not now

Hush now, I know what to do.
Find the place that always waits.
Is there sand there? Bury yourself deep
in its sun-stores. Lie there as long
as it takes. Are there waves?
Let them dump you. Is there a creek?
Sit and listen. Smell its closeness
to your body, the intimate trickle
of water through leaf-rot. Is there snow?
Fall into it, face down. Feel its aristocratic slap,
the clarity of its sting. Are there mountains?
Climb them, press your body against
the rock's indifference. Is there a river?
Stand in it. Wrestle for your footing.
Feel its urgency, its desire for you.
Are there hills? Walk your feet
all over them, smell the brawny reek
of sheep dung, lock your ear to the whirr
of the wire fence in the wind.
Now – are you here? are you here?

because the world can do that to you

and if the world did do that to you,
and took me from you, before the time
was true and right and before we all had time
to see the things and do the things and tell
the things we need to tell, to see, to do,
so many things I cannot even imagine them

because you are only six,
and your mind is crowded with soccer and cricket
and deep-sea life, with knights and Narnia
and the thermohaline conveyor, and when you were five
you cried inconsolably for forty-five minutes
when the All Blacks lost, and already when you read
you cannot hear my voice, and you are fierce
and deep and I am afraid for you

and because you are only two and three-quarters
and your heart is full of trains and racing cars
and tigers and Tiggers and dinosaurs, and when
you jump into the pool with your water-wings on
your face explodes with surprise and joy, every
single time, and you are tough and resilient
and cheeky as hell but you still need to know
where I am, about every three minutes

and because you are only nearly one and your mind
is full of god knows what – sticky things, shiny things,
soft things, loud things, faces and brothers and chuckles
and screams, and every time you lie drinking
your bottle by yourself I think of all the times

I wasn't there, of how they rushed you into life
like there wasn't enough time in the world,

which there isn't, sometimes

so if the world did do that to you
and took me from you, before the time
was true and right and before we all had time
to do the things we need to do, to fight more
and laugh more and be bored together
over and over, to ease into the big questions
slowly, not all at once, not like that,

like a trapdoor opening up
under your feet
and a sickening drop

but if the world did do that to you
I have to think that you would be

all right

after all

Matakawau

when the sea pulls this far out
the world is simply tender

the mudflats gleam,
shellfish click and gurgle

birds call out across
a barely possible openness

the sand seeps and mutters,
chuckles to itself

as it sees the sky again,
bashful of its pleasure

in bareness, of its longing
for the moment

when the tide turns
and the water comes again

so cold
so clean